HUSH

SIDAANTI SINGLA

Made with ♥ on the Notion Press Platform
www.notionpress.com

To every woman because you deserve better.

Contents

Contents

PREFACE

I would like to thanks my mom for always encouraging me and never doubted my capabilites. Its because of her I am blessed to live my life with no fear and always supporting me to look forward in my life.

Secondaly to my college teachers for helping me in completion of this book. Thanks for making out time for the contribution. You all will have a speacial place in my heart.

Last but not the least to every perosn out there who has been supporting and understaning women so that they can live their life peacefully and with her choices and rights.

List Of Contributors

- PANKAJ KUMAR GARG

  (principal)

- DR. NAVJOT KAUR

  (Incharge Academics)

- DR. NIRMAL KAUR

  (Assistant Prof. In Law)

- PANKAJ SAHOTRA

  (Assistant Prof. In Law)

- SANCHI SINLA

"स्त्रीरत्न के समान और कोई रत्न नही हौ

There is no jewel like a woman."

I
Introduction

You have read the title of the book 'HUSH' and of course, must have heard it somewhere right! It's used when you are asked to silence yourself. It also means that for that moment you are not allowed to speak or utter any word. This indicates that for that particular moment you are under the control of that person who is controlling your right to speak for that period and we usually see that in the library, hospitals, places of worship, or any other. But yeah not to forget we usually observe silence in at hunted areas too where a single sound can make you skip a beat.

People speak up whenever they want to where ever they want to. Nobody controls them at all. They speak for good, for bad, for themselves, or sometimes about others which we call Gossips. They express their thoughts, feelings, emotions, talk about new ideas and then discuss them. They do what they want to do or what they feel like doing. Nobody controls anyone's actions or words.

But just imagine what if someone asked to remain quiet and you have to remain under the control of that person and ask you to do whatever they think you should do and you shouldn't. They control your voice and words according to their mind. They control your lifestyle according to their wish. They chose your circle and even they control with whom you wish to spend your whole with!!

What will you do at that time? You will shout but you can't. You will argue but you can't do that either. You will beg but aren't they controlling you! You will run but they are the ones who will tell you with whom you have to!. So what are you gonna do now ??

Sounds too restrictive or trapped right. Seems like you have no choice but to survive because you have to and in some worse scenarios you are surviving because you are not allowed to die too!!

What do you think of living a life like that? Does it seems like living like a human being!? Not at all right. Seems to live more like a human slave and that without any pay.

Do you ever choose this life for yourself? No doubt your answer would be NO. But still, some choose to build this form of life for others. They put thousands of restrictions over them, making them see the cruel side of the world without knowing what the reality is and letting them believe that this is how they have to live from now.

They become the victim of time, society, and evil-minded people. It's so because society views them as the victims or the weaker part of the society but their only wrong is that they are WOMEN.

Yes, it's women who face all of it during their lifetime, and still, they are not allowed to utter or share anything with others. They are made to remain under the control of their parents and then their husbands and in-laws. They do live their whole life under pressure mentally, emotionally, physically, and not to forget sometimes sexually.

They face it all by themselves and if they chose to step out of it and wish to see what the outer world looks like they are made to believe that it was their bad choice to make. They are being locked up in their house or room. They started to get questions about their character. Their family starts being judged and by the time a woman could think of anything else for her their right to education has already been taken without letting them know.

They make her feel like in prison but the irony is at her place which should feel like paradise for her. Her parents or family members play the role well of a wretch who can make her life miserable enough to believe that there is something wrong with her or her mind which made such a decision.

Without giving it second thought every single girl out there has once or least has brought this thought in their minds that why they are girls and why aren't they boys? What aren't they allowed to do all the stuff which boys do? Why do they are considered a weaker part of society? Why all the restrictions which are made are only for them? And many more surely.

But do you who made them think like this about themselves, its Society with a narrow mindset. They believe that a woman must just look after her house, children, and husband. They don't let her think for herself and nothing beyond that. They restrict her thinking capacity by everyday bullying, taunting, shouting, beating, judging, and by making her believe in less for her.

Why all this to her? What wrong does she has done to anyone out there? We all can hear and talk about the wrongful act committed against her but do we ever decide to change the happening. No, rather than this we make our daughters look at it carefully as a warning example so that if ever in future she did any mistake then the same is going to happen with her.

In kindergarten, we get our girls dressed up in princesses with her crown or butterflies and make them believe that they can fly high as they want because now they have a crown which indicates that they can lead their own life, and wings that can make them fly where ever and whenever they want to.

But soon when they grow up they first take your crown back and cut your wings. That is the very first thing they take from you and you don't realize when all this happens because they are the actual masters or rulers of your life. That childhood which you believed was real rather than it ended up being just a one-time thing of your life.

It's just a matter of time a girl grows up before she could reveal what wants or feels like, she is expected to act, think, want, speak, dress up and behave according to others expectations and her own choice is buried deep down where she could never think to reach back.

Her choices get overlooked for their desires. Her wishes are taken for granted because it doesn't make any sense to them. Her pain is not felt because she demanded much. Her tears are not seen because they ask her to hide. Her words don't matter because they ask her to Hush!

That's what the title of the book and author trying to express. Women are made to silent themselves at every stage of life and they are expected to live on other terms and conditions of living.

For how long this will continue? either it is for a short period of time or just during a particular age or none of them matters but just for eternity because she is a woman?

At what stage of her life she can actually feel safe and enjoy herself being a woman. Living under constant pressure is hard for everyone but why do we tend to ignore the pressure we gave her to play her role as a person who is bound to answer and give the explanation for everything she wanted to.

We don't let her speak, don't let her express herself, and don't let her feel the way she felt. We want her to run her life we projected or society projected for her which with no doubt don't include her choices.

They are not just bound by some thoughts or perspectives. Their actions and words are also restricted or controlled by the set of rules or rituals they have been following from generation to generation. That tells her how a woman should be obeying her father's choices, how a woman is allowed to speak in front of others, her duties towards her home, society, and children. rather than helping the family financially or in business, they should be learning how to handle the kitchen, home, and looking after others' needs.

They have a different believes system they follow by projecting a woman they lure in their poems, songs, culture, traditions, films, or deities they believe in.

Those women which they perceive aren't the real ones at all. but they imagined then as they wanted her to behave and express their thoughts skillfully through different means like in romantic poems, in short stories, or in short play sometimes depicting how she managed to look after her home and husband bt ignoring her all wishes and choices, by scarifying her own will and accepting to act as a slave to keep her in-laws and husband satisfied and blissful to have her and showing how terribly the other women ended up living because she chose to go against every norm which was made to follow.

They show how bad things happen with those women who chose to handle their life own and how miserable their life can become if they chose to speak up for themselves by standing against their people.

Always they have formed the restrictive mindset of the people that now subconsciously people tend to think that this is how a woman should be behaving. They have completely forgotten about her needs, wants, desires, wishes, choices, and most importantly her consent in everything they do to her.

Notes

""Age of consent ,or a definite minimum age to engage in sexual activity, is how we measure adulthood...age boundaries are drawn more for political reasons not scientific ones."

Ram Jethmalani, jurist, 2013, in debates on rising the age of consent from 16 to 18.

"

Sexual Privacy

by:- Sanchi Singla

II

Sexual Privacy

Sex is selling. Sex rea//yseiis in the media business and in the outer worid. With their profitability in free-fall, Newspaper businesses especially are always on the lookout for a front-page story to help them grab some precious market share.

The right to engage in sexual intercourse is an intrinsic part of the right to privacy.

There are all sorts of ethical questions arising out of this, but from our point of view, it largely boils down to the question of when our sex lives should be private.

Let's sort out some of the considerations here:

Number one *CONSENT*

**Obviously the starting point here is consensual sex between adults. Forced sex or sex crimes fall into an entirely different realm of privacy.

Number two *HARMS*

**Without pubiic interest, for the equation to fall on the side of publishing, there will often have to be some meaningful moral benefits for one or more of the parties to the "private" act.

Number three *PRiVACY*

**Privacy is typically attributed when there is a reasonable expectation that something will remain so. A telephone call or a conversation in a private residence should reasonably be expected to remain private.

CONSENT!!!

Signs of consent

- Saying 'yes'

- Telling you that they are enjoying the sexual activity and want to continue

- Eye contact

- Being relaxed

- Touching or kissing you back

- Being responsive

Signs of non-consent

- Saying 'no'

- Avoiding eye contact

- Crying or shaking

- Flinching

- Resistance

- Silence or stillness

One should be respectful towards others human body. Respecting your partner's sexual privacy is of utmost importance. We can also consider the following:

- Each person's body, boundaries, and feelings are as important as the others.

- Neither person sees or treats the other iike

  they are worth less than themselves.

- Each person listens to what is being communicated, both in words and body language.

- Only doing sexual activities which both people want to do; without any force, pressure, or lies.

- Both have full capacity to consent to sexual activity — drugs and alcohol can limit capacity.

In case you sense danger...don't hesitate to call a near-dear one. Fo not engage in any activity if it's harmfui for you.
In an emergency
if you're ever in immediate harm or danger:

- the police on 100 straight away

Tell an adult you trust who will be able to support you through a difficult time

Notes

WOMEN

"I raise up my voice – not so that I can shout, but so that those without a voice can be heard. ... We cannot all succeed when half of us are held back."

Malala Yousafzai

Media

by:- Dr. Nirmal Kaur

III

Media

So far we have made enormous progress in almost all the fields representing society. In the era of globalization, media has become the buzzword. Needless to save rapid expansion of globalization had been made possible by the media (popularly known as the four pillars of democracy). It can fairly acknowledge that media has played a significant role in the promotion and dissemination of information and more importantly has been a key player in the socio-economic development of women in society. Every coin has two sides, media can also play a greater role in ethics perpetuating or challenging societal and behavioral norms that inculcate and accelerate objectification of women or violence against women.

The Revolutionanization of information and technology –is a modern phenomenon. During the last few decades the overall scenario of media and its story coverage helped changed enormously women portrait in undoubted area of concern be it daily soaps movies news items, advertisement, etc. it often seems that sexism and sensationalization is the primary motive behind the media coverage. Depiction of women in different situations has received negative comments from large straps of society because appearances of the fairer sex have violated the requirements of good taste, decency, and morality as ensured under Article 19[1](2) of the Indian constitution. The presentation of women is generally scrupulous religiously tolerant family nurturers and culturally ultra-modern. The commodification of women as sex objects is a matter of great concern.

Daily sope broadcast on Indian television enjoys immense popularity amongst the Indian masses. Soaps such as Balika Vadhu, Uttaran, Pavitar Rishta, Saas-Bahu, and many more have been watched by the majority of Indian people. These telenovels stretch over 3-4 years with hundreds of episodes and are namely broadcast nightly. The way such t.v. serials displayed are clogging the path of emancipation of women from all these orthodox traditions. These daily dramas project women as models of expensive costumes, jewelry, and more over the stereotypes used- that offer a dominating mother-in-law, a wronged wife, the bitter relationship between sister-in-law. Though they bear a close resemblance with real-life situations, have badly failed to do justice to the changing patterns of the identity of women within households. They failed to show all the career options that are now being adopted by Indian women. In the name of entertainment, such serials are deteriorating the merciful situation of Indian women.

Over the course of history, checking women's representation by media, women have been defined in very narrow roles. When women started appearing on t.v. ads people were actually dismissive of her role as a model for ads. It was indicative of the problems where women had firmly been placed in the domestic sphere, talking animatedly about cleaning and household chores. In the recent past portrayal of women has witnessed a tremendous change. Some of the ads are depicted according to the changing times advertising sector has become that major sector that affects our lives consciously and subconsciously.

It has shaped society from a much broader perspective. The majority of women are no longer confined within molded perspectives accordingly. Taking advantage of the situation the marketers have wisely utilized this chance to launch their products through advertisement strategically. Though portraying evolving gender roles has always been a hard nut to crack some brands dare to shatter the stereotypes smartly by showing causing contemporary women in their new avatars. Some of the ads, calling in this category are- ariel's share the load, where the man agrees to share the laundry duties of his wife, Titan Raga-# Her Life Her Choices, in which chow cast a strong and independent woman who is capable of talking her decisions on her own and making out her choices, the Airtel –Boss, featured a modern-day couple in which women is a multi-tasker handling her office and home smartly by juggling professional duties and personal life. Moreover, the ad for the Eco sports car shows Kalki Koechlin, taking the wheel in her own hands showing that he loves Raksha Bandhan but is no longer dependent on her brother for her safety. The ad has an undertone of feminism which was rare to get to see in Indian ads.

On the flipping side, the majority of ads still show women as a nurturer of the family, and caretakers of children despite the fact that both mother and father are the guardians of the ward. As a nurturer men weren't allowed either. Apparently, the most devastating part of the ads is where women are portrayed to justice fill the background of the scenery. They aren't supposed to be the protagonist unless the ad is for cleaning products, beauty brands, and other household chores which are gender specific. Not only this some ads have represented women in such a derogatory way violating the standards of morality and decency.

Coming to the cinema, for centuries, Indian Hindi cinema has become a platform to give impetus to Indian history and culture. it has gracefully expressed the changing trends of tradition. India leading up to modern India which no other art form has done so far. The Bollywood industry tries to identify those aspects where modern feminism connects with traditional moral and social values. The big screen has also largely been inspired by religion and mythology where females were seen as the epitome of virtue and values who could commit no wrongdoings. For instance, the character of Sita, Draupatti has been noticed in many films repeatedly. Over time, movies have come to the rescue of women by filming them in such a way that has shattered the stereotypes retained of women.

Now cinema has come a long way in creating a success story. how can we forget the roles played by Meena Kumari in Sahib Bibi Aur Ghulam(1962), and Waheed Rehmaan in Guide(1957). in addition to it even the roles played by Kajol in Dilwale Dhulhania Le Jayenge(1995), Priyanka Chopra in Fashion(2008), Vidya Balan in Begum Jaan(2017) Aliya Bhatt in Gangu Bai Kathiawadi(2022) are commendable. In spite of the fact that such blockbusters have changed the whole scenario and increased accessibility of such films, the plight of Indian women has not changed much, because objectification of women is still the same in many of the movies in the shape of item numbers, cameo performances or for merely loving making scenes. It's a matter of surprise how the censor board approves of the commodification of women in many films.

It does not end here, in Bollywood movies a female actor will not be offered roles in the lead if she gets married or have kids or gets aged. However, the same is not true in the case of male heroes. They will remain heroes even in there in the '50s or '60s will be placed against a 20-year-old heroine. Our Bollywood industry is flooded with such examples.

Besides all the above, the honesty of the internet and social media platforms namely Instagram, Facebook, Twitter, Snapchat, etc. have broadened and widened the social space for females to raise their matters. These platforms have certainly provided the impetus for the empowerment of women through advanced technology.

However, at the very same time, a digital divide based on gender is creating an unequal face in digital media as well; the reasons for this could be social, economic, and personal. According to the united nation broadband commission for digital development, 73% of women have encountered cyber violence; they received death, rape threats, and abuses for expressing themselves online. According to a UN survey on women, 23% of women have faced online abuse and consequently withdrawn themselves from social media and stopped posting on specific issues on different online handles. Cyber crimes against women such as online stalking sending unsolicited messages on Whats app and E-mail, creating pornography, and morphed content targeting women are some of the instances of harassment of women on social media. Her woes are further increased when she doesn't know where to report the commission of these cyber crimes.

Notes

""When women are educated, their countries
become stronger and more prosperous."
Michelle Obama"

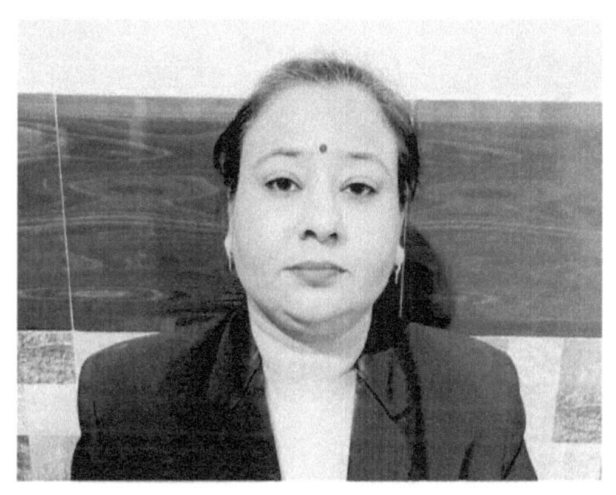

Education

by Dr. Navjot Kaur

IV

Education

The Right to Education has been recognised as an integral and essential part for every person irrespective of gender. Historically, education for men was promoted in all cultures, while women's education was not considered important or necessary. Gender discrimination at all levels and the perception that women need not be educated persisted even when men all over the world were being educated as doctors, engineers, lawyers, etc. To overturn this social dogma, women have fought for their right to education for almost 200 years now. Through countless debates and endless movements all over the world, men and women fought the long battle for women's education. Women are the indispensable part of a society. Their education influence the coming generation.The development of future generation mainly depends upon the education of women section.So the education of women is realized to be the most essential part for the development of the society. It can help every woman to educate their children to be good manager of the family as well as the active member of the society. The children learn their manners and behaviour at home and mostly mothers are responsible for cultivating good behaviour in their children .Every educated woman can run her house well and make it a paradise on earth.Every educated woman can think well about her future and her aim in life and then choose the appropriate subject which will be useful to her throughout the life. In a democratic system, the position of women is equal to that of men.Nowadays women are also conscious about their rights and obligations.[1] Women and men are equally treated in the eyes of the law. However, our cultural conditioning is the main source of atrocities against women. Culturally, a woman in India is supposed to remain confined at home for internal domestic routine work and men on the other hand is the bread earner. However, due to the spread of education a lot of changes could be observed. In light of the needs and importance of women's education, a study is undertaken, entitled as "Development of women's education in Darrang District since independence."

Women play a very important role in the progress of a family, society and country. In order to make democracy successful in the country women education is necessary together with the men. Educated women are the real source of happiness in the family. Education is one of the milestones for women empowerment because it enables them to respond to the challenges, to confront their traditional role and change their life-style. Nowadays, the importance of women's education is growing day by day. It is not only important to educate girls and women, but also it is necessary to provide them with basic facilities. In many countries, especially in developing countries, the literacy rate of women is low compared to men. The main reason behind this illiteracy rate among women is the lack of proper resources. Women's Education in India, the situation of women's education is not very good. According to the 2011 census, the literacy rate of Indian women was 64.6%. This number is quite low compared to the literacy rate of men, which is 80.9%. [2]

v. HISTORY OF WOMEN'S EDUCATION IN INDIA

Women around the world, and especially in Indian society, have long been subject to the discrimination and tortures inflicted by the so-called patriarchal society. Women have always been considered the weaker section of society, and hence made to believe in male supremacy. They were always expected to be obedient to the male gender, expected to serve the male gender, were silenced when they were subject to violence by those men. A woman who obediently went through all of this without voicing her opinion was deemed to be fit for society or else, termed as uncultured and shamed for her mere existence.

Women's education in India plays a very important role in the overall development of the country. It not only helps in the development of half of the human resources, but in improving the quality of life at home and outside.

Although in the Vedic period women had access to education in India, they gradually lost this right. However, in the British period there was revival of interest in women's education in India. During this period, various socio religious movements led by eminent persons like Raja Ram Mohan Roy, Iswar Chandra Vidyasagar emphasized on women's education in India.

Mahatma JyotibaPhule, Periyar, and Baba Saheb Ambedkar were leaders of the lower castes in India who took various initiatives to make education available to the women of India. However women's education got a fillip after the country got independence in 1947 and After India attained independence in 1947, the University Education Commission was created to recommend suggestions to improve the quality of education. However, their report spoke against female education, referring to it as: "Women's present education is entirely irrelevant to the life they have to lead. It is not only a waste but often a definite disability."

However, the fact that the female literacy rate was at 8.9% post-Independence could not be ignored. Thus, in 1958, a national committee on women's education was appointed by the government, and most of its recommendations were accepted. The crux of its recommendations were to bring female education on the same footing as offered for boys.Soon afterward, committees were created that talked about equality between men and women in the field of education. For example, one committee on differentiation of curriculum for boys and girls (1959) recommended equality and a common curricula at various stages of their learning. Further efforts were made to expand the education system, and the Education Commission was set up in 1964, which largely talked about female education, and recommended a national policy to be developed by the government. This occurred in 1968, providing increased emphasis on female education.[3]

As a result, women's literacy rate has grown over the three decades and the growth of female literacy has in fact been higher than that of male literacy rate. While in 1971 only 22% of Indian women were literate, by the end of 2001 54.16% of females were literate. The growth of female literacy rate is 14.87% as compared to 11.72 % of that of male literacy rate.

V. UNDERLYING CAUSES OF WOMEN'S EDUCATION

- **Poverty and Entrenched Patriarchy**: Entrenched patriarchy and deep-rooted gender biases in society affects education of girls. Regressive gender norms places the unpaid care burden on girls with sibling care, household chores invariably been seen as their responsibility. Patriarchal social norms like child marriage and dowry restrictions on the mobility of girls act as barriers to education of girls. India witnesses the highest number of female infanticides and the discrimination persists in the form of poor nutrition, Gender-based violence (GBV), and early marriage.

- **Safety and Security of Girls** at home, school and community is a major issue. Entrenched patriarchy and unequal gender norms and power relations which drive violence against girls and manifest themselves as bullying and physical abuse, corporal punishment, sexual and verbal harassment, non-consensual touching and other forms of sexual assault.

- **Systemic Factors**: Issues like lack of conducive infrastructure, poor quality of education, lack of women teachers, poor linkages to upper primary schools, lack of sensitised teachers, curriculum that is not gender-responsive often compel girls to either leave school or fail to attain the desired learning competencies. The lack of separate functional toilets for girls, as lack of proper infrastructure, makes girls even more vulnerable. Lack of menstrual knowledge, along with a non-conducive school infrastructure and lack of sanitary products, often compel girls to remain at home.

- **Intersectionality of gender, region, social class and religion affects**: Girls from Scheduled Caste (SC) and Scheduled Tribe (ST) or Muslim communities are subject to multiple marginalization.20 Patriarchy amplifies discriminatory practices rooted in prejudice against the marginalized communities, hence girls suffer doubly, because they are girls and more so because they are from an oppressed community.[4]

The Right to Education Act in India was a major turning point for school education, it made education a fundamental right for children in the age group 6 to 14. The Act brought positive changes in the school education system which also benefitted girls. Through Sarva Shiksha Abhiyan, the umbrella scheme for implementation of the RTE Act, critical barriers like access and inclusion were addressed to a large extent, which led to increasing in enrolment at both the primary and upper primary levels. Along with this, schemes like RashtriyaMadhyamikShikshaAbhiyan and National Scheme of Incentives to Girls for Secondary Education emphasized secondary education of girls through scholarships, subsidies and incentives. With the introduction of BetiBachaoBetiPadhao in 2014 a renewed emphasis was given to education of girls. However, girls' participation in secondary and higher secondary education, and stark regional and social group disparities remain areas of grave concern

v. **SIGNIFICANCE OR BENEFITS OF WOMEN'S EDUCATION**

- Educating the women will empower them to seek gender equality in the society.
- Women will be able to earn which would raise their economic condition and their status in society.

- They will be aware of the advantages of small and planned families and this will be a big step towards achieving stabilized population goals.
- Girls need to be educated because it is their Right, it is their basic entitlement. Education is 'a sure way of giving them much greater power -- of enabling them to make genuine choices over the kinds of lives they wish to lead
- Educated girls will have skills, information and self-confidence that helps her be a better worker, citizen and a parent.
- Education transforms lives of girls, she is safer, is better nourished, experiences less discrimination, makes her own decisions and has control on her productive and reproductive life.
- Education helps girls to play a leadership role in their community and society at large.
- It has been reported that the single most important factor affecting high total fertility rates (TFR) is the low status of women in many societies. Women education will help increase the age of marriage of women and they would tend to have fewer, healthier children who would live longer.[5]
- Women on being educated would be able to rear their children in a better way, leading to their good health and provide them with better facilities.
- Women are also the victim of capitalism and development. Due to some development activity like dam building or mining, they get rehabilitated. The men folk get some compensation and migrate to towns in search of some job while women are left behind to look after the family with little resources. They are compelled to take up some marginalized work, which is highly

unorganized and often socially humiliating. Women's education can greatly help restore their settlement and dignity.

- Education of women would mean narrowing down social disparities and inequities. This would automatically lead to sustainable development.[6]

v. WOMEN AND THE RIGHT TO EDUCATION

- In accordance with Article 26 of the Universal Declaration of Human Rights, "Everyone has the right to education".
- Article 3 of the International Covenant on Economic, Social and Cultural Rights requires States parties to undertake "to ensure the equal right of men and women to the enjoyment of all economic, social and cultural rights" set forth in that treaty, including the right to education.
- Article 13 of the International Covenant on Economic, Social and Cultural Rights provides "the right of everyone to education. " To this end, "primary education shall be compulsory and available free to all". Secondary education in its different forms, including technical and vocational secondary education, and higher education, on the basis of capacity, shall be made generally and equally accessible to all, and in particular by the progressive introduction of free education.
- Article 5 of the <u>Convention on the Elimination of All Forms of Racial Discrimination</u> provides"States Parties undertake to prohibit and to eliminate racial discrimination and to guarantee the right of everyone, without distinction as to race, color, or national or ethnic origin, to equality before the law ... in the

enjoyment of ... the right to education and training.."[7]

- Articles 3 and 4 of the Convention Against Discrimination in Education provide "The States Parties undertake to discontinue any practices which involve discrimination in education to develop a national policy which will promote equality of opportunity and of treatment in education and in particular: To make primary education free and compulsory; make secondary education available and accessible to all; make higher education equally accessible to all on the basis of individual capacity; assure compliance by all with the obligation to attend school prescribed by law; To encourage and intensify the education of persons who have not received any primary education or who have not completed the entire primary education.. "

- Article 28 of the Convention on the Rights of the Child provides, inter alia, that States Parties shall "make primary education compulsory and available free to all", "make higher education accessible to all on the basis of capacity by every appropriate means", and "take measures to encourage regular attendance at schools and the reduction of drop-out rates."

- Article 10 of the Convention on the Elimination of All Forms of Discrimination against Women, details a number of measures which should be taken to eliminate discrimination against women in order to ensure to them equal rights with men in the field of education.

- UNESCO Convention against Discrimination in Education also bans discrimination in education on the basis of sex, referring to all types and levels of education, and includes access to education, the standard and quality of education, and the conditions under which it is given.

- The Beijing Platform of Action of the UN Fourth World Conference on Women in 1995 recognized education as a basic human right and an essential tool for achieving more equal relations between women and men. States committed to ensuring a number of strategic objectives, including: equal access to education, the closing of the gender gap in primary and secondary education, and development of non-discriminatory education and training by developing and using curriculums, textbooks and teaching aids free of sex-stereotyping.
- Millennium Development Goal 2 calls for universal primary education. MDG 3 to "Promote Gender Equality and Empower Women", has as one of its targets: "Eliminate gender disparity in primary and secondary education, preferably by 2005, and in all levels of education no later than 2015".[8]

The right to education is the entitlement to access free primary education, and to have equal opportunities to continue with further study. Such education must be inclusive and accessible to girls and boys, women and men, in law and in practice. Education is not only a right in itself, but is also the surest way to empower individuals to enjoy all of their human rights. Education paves the way out of poverty and disempowerment and opens up access to participation in society and in political decision-making.[9] Women and girls have historically suffered discrimination in the area of education, and continue to do so in many places of the world. Progress has been made in narrowing gender gaps in education over the past decade, in particular at the primary level. However, girls' secondary school enrolment has increased at a much slower rate and is widening in some regions. The largest disparities are found in sub-Saharan Africa, South and West Asia, Central Asia, and the Arab States. Within countries, significant inequalities can be found related to language, ethnicity, or social status. According to official UN statistics, of the estimated 72 million children who are not in school, girls are the majority. Girls are less likely than boys to be in school, and more likely than boys never to be Enrolled. In contrast in terms of grade repetition, boys are more likely than girls to repeat primary grades in most countries where such data exists.

The Indian Constitution has time and again propagated the values of equality among the citizens and has empowered women in all social, cultural, and economic spheres. It prohibits discrimination based on caste, religion, sex, etc. These laws were enacted for the upliftment of women so that they live honorable and dignified life. Only when a woman has equal occupational rights, educational rights, decision-making rights, freedom and the right to choose what's good for herself, she is said to be equal to that of men. Gender equality is the essence of the Indian Constitution and thus, the following are the laws enacted for the protection of women's rights.[10]

v. **CONCLUSION**

Women's education plays an imperative role in making a nation progressive and guiding it toward development. It is necessary to provide girls and women with proper resources so that they can get educated. Girls and women have the potential to contribute to the economic development of their countries. They can also play an important role in the development of their families. Therefore, it is necessary to pay more attention to women's education. Since 1986, many important changes and a new approach to education especially in terms of early childhood and primary schooling have been brought. The new education policy of 2020, pledges to break the gender barriers and make education available to all. The higher education system has been fragmented and has recommended adopting a more holistic approach to address 21st-century goals. We hope this will now build an overarching structure allowing more flexibility and integration in learning. Where at the one hand the new policy recommends studying science in regional languages on the other hand the policy is trying to make online education a natural part of the system to make it more robust. We have happily arrived at a juncture today where education is regarded as a basic human right. However, we are still a long way from ensuring that this right is available and implemented to every single person in our ever developing world.[11]

* Asstt. Prof. in Law, Baba Farid Law College, Faridkot.

[1]Introduction, *available at:* http://shodh.inflibnet.ac.in:8080/jspui/bitstream/123456789/41/2/02_chapters.pdf (last visited on July 03, 2022).

[2] Introduction on Women's Education, *available at:*https://www.vedantu.com/english/women-education-in-india-essay (last visited on July 03, 2022).

[3] Post-Independence Educational Development among women in India, *available at:* https://web.archive.org/web/20130222012631/http://www.cwds.ac.in/OCPaper/Post-IndependenceEducational.pdf (last visited on July 5, 2022).

[4] Policy Brief on Girl education, *available at:* https://www.careindia.org/wp-content/uploads/2021/05/Policy-Brief-Girls-Education.pdf (last visited on July 5, 2022).

[5]Bhat T. "Women Education in India Need of the Ever". Human Rights International research journal: Vol. 1 p.3 (2014).

[6] The History of Women's Education in India, *available at:* https://www.yourarticlelibrary.com/education/the-history-of-womens-education-in-india/9982 (last visited on July 5, 2022).

[7] Women, human rights and education, *available at:* https://www.pdhre.org/rights/women_and_education.html (last visited on July 6, 2022).

[8] Women and the right to education, *available at:* https://www.ohchr.org/sites/default/files/Documents/Issues/Women/GenderAndEquality/Infonote_Women_and_the_right_to_education.pdf (last visited on July 5, 2022).

[9] Women and Girls, *available at:* https://www.right-to-education.org/girlswomen (last visited on July 5, 2022).

[10] Women Laws in India, *available at:*https://www.legalserviceindia.com/legal/article-6618-women-laws-in-india.html (last visited on July 5, 2022).

[11] Importance of education for women, *available at:* https://infinitylearn.com/surge/english/article/importance-of-education-for-women/ (last visited on July 6, 2022).

Notes

"*"For me, a better democracy is a democracy where women do not only have the right to vote and to elect but to be elected." - Michele Bachelet*"

Politics

By:- Pankaj Kumar Garg

&

by:- Pankaj Sahotra

V
Politics

Revisiting of Women's right in Politics - An Overview

The political empowerment of women is a social process crucial to development and progress. The status of women is measured internationally by the participation of women in politics and their empowerment. Women remain seriously underrepresented in decision-making positions. To empower women legislation was proposed to reserve $1/3^{rd}$ of seats in the Parliament and State Legislatures for women. It was drafted first by the H D Deve Gowda-led United Front government and introduced in Lok Sabha in 1996. Although it has been introduced in Parliament several times, the Bill could not be passed because of a lack of political consensus. The 73rd Amendment Act, in the Panchayati Raj system, provides for 33% reservation for women in all three tiers. It is a step towards removing the inequality and incapability of women in all tiers of government. Art,14,15,16,39(a)(c),42,325,326,243D back the women's representation in politics. In 2018 Spain's King Felipe VI swore in the country's new government led by Prime Minister Pedro Sánchez. It was a moment of some significance: Out of 17 ministers in Sánchez's cabinet, 11 were women. This is, by far, the most in the country's history. It is, in fact, the most female cabinet in Europe. This is not an incidental fact or mere symbolism. B.R. Ambedkar once said that "political power is the key to all social progress". What, then, to make of the fact that India—a country where women suffer substantially greater socio-economic disadvantages and face very less representation of women in politics? Many democratic countries today are faced with the challenge of increasing women's presence in public life and other key decision-making roles.- In the 2019 general election out of the total 29 states, women MPs were elected only from 22 states. And seven states had no female representation in the parliament. The seven states were Arunachal Pradesh, Himachal Pradesh, Jammu and Kashmir, Manipur, Mizoram, Nagaland, and Sikkim. Uttar Pradesh and West Bengal elected the highest number of women MPs, with 11 candidates each. Out of National political parties, the BJP had a maximum number of winning women MPs at 41. (News 18, 2019). While the 2019 general election witnessed the highest representation of women in LokSabha, still the equal representation of women in Parliament still has a long way to go.

This chapter aims to examine the current laws and legislations related to the political participation of women along with other laws that are in favor of the same. It also takes into consideration various aspects such as history and the global scenario to deal with the political participation of women in India; that is the contribution of great leaders. It also talks about the problems faced by women in getting equal political participation as men. It also addresses the various contributing factors such as lack of education and awareness, poverty, the institution of marriage, and the mindset of the people.

Introduction

'It is very difficult for a woman to make up her mind to enter politics. Once she makes up her own mind, then she has to prepare her husband, her children, and her family. Once she has overcome all these obstacles and applies for the ticket, then the male aspirants against whom she is applying make up all sorts of stories about her. And after all, this, when her name goes to the party bosses, they do not select her name because they fear losing that seat.'The above quote by SushmaSwaraj (Union External Affairs Minister) gives a glimpse of the reality that how women have to face so many problems and criticisms while entering politics.

Politics involves representation, policy, power, and position with Government as its area. Political participation refers to the participation of individuals in the political process. It ensures that individuals are able to take part in deciding the common goals of society and the best ways of achieving them. Political participation means not merely exercising the right to vote, but also power sharing, decision-making, and policy-making at all levels of governance of the State. Political participation refers to actual participation in these voluntary activities by which the members of the society share in the selection of rules and formulation of public policy directly or indirectly.

Political participation of women in any country gives an overview of how women are treated in society. The development of any country also depends on the equal participation of men and women. Since women's presence is seemed to be low in Indian politics, it is the duty of every human being to make them aware of their rights and motivate them for participating in mainstream politics. The constitution of India not only guarantees equality in society but also suggests states make special provisions for women. Women still are fighting for equal status in society. Because of their low representation in Indian politics, their issues and problems are generally unseen and unnoticed. Their genuine demands are not raised before the decision-makers. Women need to be dependent to make their own decisions.

It is the need of the hour in a country like India to have equal participation of women in mainstream political activity. Society needs to deconstruct the stereotype of women as limited to household activities only. The nature of society has a crucial impact on the extent and effectiveness of women's political participation. Their low representation in decision making

History of the rise of women

The roots of the present always lie in the past. So, the justification of the law relating to the political participation of women can be appropriately scrutinized only by looking into the past history of any system. The way to shed some light on women's right to political participation is to look at its past at the national as well as global levels. If we see the international history of women's political participation, the history of equal participation of women in the political fields in a few countries, it can be observed that in ancient Greece and Republican Rome as well as in a few more democracies have emerged in Europe, women were completely not given voting rights by the end of the 18th century. In the United States of America, women in this country were the first ones to fight for their right to vote in the whole world. If we see the Indian history, women have a record of suffering and exploitation. The women have remained victims of violence and also, and they have suffered various types of discrimination, exploitation, and torture- both physical and mental not only in the men's society but also within their own house by their family thereby disturbing the balance in the society. Before Independence, Local Self-Governments existed in India since. Vedas, Puranas, Smritis, and books on statecrafts and religious texts have vivid descriptions of this. In the past, the Panchayati Raj system was confined to solving social problems with the help of five senior members of a village called 'Pinchas'. The fact that women are capable of exhibiting extraordinary qualities of leadership is visible by the participation of many women during the national freedom movement. There were many women who fought during the freedom struggle but some of them who were prominent women were Sarojini Naidu, Kamala Devi Chattopadhyay, SuchetaKriplani, Aruna Asif Ali, Kasturba Gandhi, and Kamala Nehru. They stand out prominently for their leadership skills. The demand for women's voting rights was initiated by Sarojini Naidu who led a delegation of Indian Women before the British Parliament in the year 1917. Consulting the Reforms Act of 1921 women were given the right to vote, but this right came with certain restrictions like wifehood, property, and education. The Government of India Act of 1935 granted voting rights to all women without any conditions as was there in the Reforms Act of 1921. Finally, the Constitution of India in the year of 1950 gave all women equal political and legal rights

Role of women in the national struggle for freedom

Women in India entered the political process in the early decades of the present century, through their massive participation in the national struggle for freedom under the leadership of Mahatma Gandhi. The first session of the Indian National Congress was attended by six women delegates. Women played a crucial role in the Swadeshi Boycott movement. Gandhi was instrumental in bringing women to the forefront of the Non-Cooperation movement. Women took an active part in boycotting foreign goods, picketing in schools, colleges, and courts, organizing processions, and spinning wheels (charka). During the Civil Disobedience Movement women in large numbers took part in the 'Dandi March' led by Gandhiji and directly participated in making salt out of seawater. Thousands of women and girls students took an active part in the Quit India movement of 1942. (Ghosh 2010) Immediately after the passing of the Quit India resolution, women leaders like Sarojini Naidu, Amrit Kaur, Rameswari Nehru, and others were taken into custody. Women were also part and parcel of the revolutionary activities of the extremist section of the freedom fighters who believed in the forcible overthrow of the British Raj. Sister Nivedita, Sarala Devi Choudharani, and Madam Bhikaji Kama were prominent among the women revolutionaries. There were around 1500 women soldiers in the Rani Jhansi Regiment of 'Azad Hind Fouz' prominent among them were Commander Lakshmi Swaminatha, Janaki Davar, and Mayawati Arya. (Sinha 2006) Indian women were also fighting for their right to vote and right to get elected in the legislature. In 1917, even before the women in England got their right to vote, Sarojini Naidu in a petition to the British parliament demanded voting rights for Indian women. By 1929, all the provincial legislatures in India guaranteed women the right to vote at par with men. The Karachi session of the Indian National Congress in 1931 accepted women there were many women organizations that played a prominent role like Nari Satyagraha Samiti and SatyagrahiSevaka Dal organized processions and violated the salt law.

Organizations like women`s Swadeshi League and DeshSevika, RashtriyaStree Sangha were quite active. The Freedom Movement and Indian women`s widespread participation in it thus brought out a conducive climate for perceptible changes in many areas. Women`s education and participation in work outside the home and in income generation were some of the changes which came out.

Constitutional Provisions for Women-

The Preamble of the Constitution of India guarantees –Justice, Liberty, and Equality to all its citizens. Constitution provides for the equality of women and called State to take measures to neutralize the socio-economic, educational, and political disadvantages faced by women.

Article 14 guarantees equality before the law and equal protection of the law within the territory of India.

Article 15 prohibits discrimination on the basis of religion, race, caste, sex, or place of birth.

Article 15(3) State can make special provisions for the benefit of women and childrenfor securing the health and strength of men and women and not to abuse the tender age of children.

Article 325 and 326 guarantees political equality, equal right to participate in the political activity and right to vote, respectively.

Article 243 (D) provides for the political reservation to women in every panchayat election, it has extended this reservation to elected office as well. (Chadha 2014)But it is really unfortunate that what is assured in the constitution is not actually realised in the day to day affairs of our country. It is, therefore, felt necessary to make special legal provisions for women in accordance with the spirit of the provisions laid down in the clause (3) of Article 15 of the constitution. The demand for greater representation of women in political institutions in India was taken up seriously after the report of the Committee on the Status of Women in India. It suggested that female representation in political institutions, especially at the grass-roots level needed to be increased through a policy of reservation of seats for women. In 1988, the National Perspective Plan for women in its first draft suggested that 30 percent reservation be provided for women from panchayat to parliament, but later in its final draft restricted the reservation to the panchayat level. The national consensus around this demand resulted in the adoption of the 73rd and 74th constitutional amendments in 1993 that provided 33 percent reservation in institutions of local governance.(Rai, 2011) This has been implemented in all states of India without any opposition. Panchayath Raj Institutions have brought about significant changes in the lives of women, The Panchayath villages have become a political training ground for women, who have become self-confident and politically aware and are transforming local governance by sensitizing the state to issues of poverty, inequality, and gender injustice. But the constitution (Eighty-first Amendment bill), popularly known as Women`s Reservation Bill which was tabled in the Lok Sabha on 12th September 1996, raised opposition from several political parties regarding issues of elitism and overlapping quotas for women generally and for lower caste women, and the bill introduced twenty-three years ago is yet to be passed.(Mandal 2003).

Women in Decision-making positions in India

Women`s participation in the decision-making process is vital to sustaining democracy. This fact was realized at the UN convention on the political rights of women in 1952. All congresses worldwide emphasized the need for the political participation of women. They discussed and planned strategies to achieve this objective. Significant deliberation on women's empowerment was made in (a) the World Plan of Action in (1975) in Mexico; (b) The Copenhagen Programme of Action (1980) (c) the World Conference on the UN Decade of Women in Nairobi (1985) and (d) the World Congress of Women in Beijing (1995). (Fadia, 2014)In 2015, September, the member states of the United Nations unanimously adopted a new global agenda to end poverty by 2030

The 2030 Agenda for Sustainable Development (SDGs) includes a specific goal to achieve gender equality, which aims to end discrimination and violence against women and girls and ensure equal participation and opportunity in all spheres of life. The target to achieve this goal is through women's full and effective participation and equal opportunities for leadership at all levels of decision-making in political, economic, and public life. (UN-Women) Sarojini Naidu was the first lady Governor of the Republic of India. She held the office from 1947 to 1949. Smt. VijayalakshmiPandit was the Governor of Maharashtra from 1962 to 1964. She was also India's Ambassador to the USSR during 1947 -1949 and President of the UN General Assembly in 1954.

Indira Gandhi was a bold key decision-maker and her decisions had a great impact on the Indian political system. She personalized and centralized politics. During her regime, the constitutional system of India became the Prime Ministerial system. Through her decisions, she eroded the federal system in India. The late, the 1980s and 1990s witnessed the emergence of women political leaders who influenced political decision-making at the national and state level.

Jayalalitha emerged as a powerful Chief Minister of Tamil Nadu after the death of M. G. Ramachandra. Jayalalitha`s AIADMK party became the principal ally of the BJP-led government in 1998. On the Cauvery issue, the AIADMK warned Prime Minister Vajpayee of "disastrous consequences" if his government did not notify immediately of the scheme on Cauvery water in the official gazette and table it in parliament. Jayalalitha withdrew her 18 MPs' support from the government after the Union cabinet rejected outright her demands to reinstate former naval chief Vishnu Bhagwat.

Mayawati is one of the most dynamic Dalit leaders. She became the first women Dalit chief minister in the year 1995. She focused on social welfare measures for the upliftment of 'Bhahujans' – other backward classes, Schedule caste, and Schedule tribes. Mayawati`s rise from a humble beginning was referred as a 'miracle of democracy' by former Prime Minister of India, P.V. Narasimha Rao. She was instrumental in toppling Vajpayee`s government in 1999, by the lowest margin of just one vote.

Mamta Banerji- Mamta Banerji is a firebrand leader. Mamta split vertically the Congress (I) in West Bengal on August 9, 1997. She claimed her Trinamul Congress was the real Congress. In the 1984 general election, Banerji became one of India`s youngest parliamentarians defeating veteran Communist politician Somnath Chatterjee. In 2011, Banerji won a sweeping majority which ended the 34 years of rule of the Left Front and she became the Ch In the 2000s the women who came to prominence were Sonia Gandhi, SushmaSwaraj, NirmalaSitharam, and SmritiIrani.

SushmaSwaraj- In March 1998, Under Prime minister Vajpayee, she was sworn in as Union Cabinet minister for Information and Broadcasting with an additional charge of the ministry of Telecommunication. She was the leader of the opposition in the 15th loksabha. She served as Minister of External Affairs under Prime Minister Narendra Modi from May 2014 to May 2019.

SmritiIrani – She is currently the youngest minister in the council of Ministers at the age of 43. She defeated Rahul Gandhi- President of the Indian National Congress in the 2019 general election. She is serving as Minister of Textiles and given additional charge as Minister of Women and Child Development.

NirmalaSitharaman- She is a member of the Rajya Sabha. In 2014 she served as the Defence Minister of India and in 2019 she became Finance Minister, the second female finance minister after Indira Gandhi.

PrathibhaPatil- She was the 12th President of India and the first women to hold that office.

SheilaDikshit was the longest serving Chief minister of Delhi for a period of 15 years.

Kiran Bedi is the first woman to join the Indian Police Service (IPS). After retirement she joined Bharatiya Janata party in January 2015. She played a key role in Indian anti-corruption movement. On 22, May 2016, she was appointed as the lieutenant Governor of Puducherry.

Meira Kumar was the Minister of Social Justice and Empowerment from 2004 to 2009.She was the 15th Speaker of LokSabhs from 2009 to 2014.Prior to being appointed as Speaker, she had been elected to the 8th,11th,12 th, and

14th, LokSabha.Sumitra Mahajan was eldest, senior most and longest serving woman Member of Parliament in the 16th, Lok Sabha. She was the second woman after Meira Kumar to be elected as the Speaker of the LokSabha.Sonia Gandhi took over as leader of Indian National Congress party in 1998, and played a prominent role in rejuvenating the dying Congress party. She was instrumental in formulating the United Progressive Alliance (UPA), which got elected for two terms in 2004 and 2009. She played an important role in passing the National Rural Employment Guarantee Scheme and the Right to Information Act. Although India has seen women participating in politics as the longest-serving Prime ministers, Chief ministers of various states, members of the national parliament, and state legislative assemblies in large numbers, the occurrence has not been corresponding to their population.

Current trends

In the 2019 general election out of the total 29 states, women MPs were elected only from 22 states. And seven states had no female representation in the parliament. The seven states were Arunachal Pradesh, Himachal Pradesh, Jammu and Kashmir, Manipur, Mizoram, Nagaland, and Sikkim. Uttar Pradesh and West Bengal elected the highest number of women MPs, with 11 candidates each. Out of National political parties, the BJP had a maximum number of winning women MPs at 41. (News 18, 2019)While the 2019 general election witnessed the highest representation of women in Lok Sabha, still the equal representation of women in Parliament still has a long way to go. Worldwide figures on the representation of women in leadership and political participation in Parliament are IJCRT2003070 International Journal of Creative Research Thoughts (IJCRT) www.ijcrt.org 554 Only 24.3 percent of all national parliamentarians were women as of 1st February 2019. (IPU-UN, Women map of Women in Politics, 2019) As of June 2019, 11 women are serving as heads of the state, and 12 are serving as heads of the Government. Rwanda has the highest number of women parliamentarians worldwide-61.3 percent seats in the lower house of the legislature, followed by Cuba with 53.2 percent and Bolivia with 53 percent. (World Economic Forum)Table 2 indicates that India has less number of women in parliament when compared to its neighboring countries like Nepal, Pakistan, Bhutan, Afghanistan, and Bangladesh. Such a dismal picture is all the more surprising because India boasts of a number of efficient and courageous women Politicians or administrators who have proved their mettle in the field of politics and administration since the early medieval period of Indian history.

OBSTACLES AND BARRIERS TO NON-PARTICIPATION OF WOMEN IN POLITICS IN INDIA

The Constitution of India gives the universal adult franchise to both men and women with equal rights to participate in electoral competition, but the existing societal value system, the private-public divide in terms of domain identification in political institutions restrict women from exercising their electoral rights and fair participation in electoral competition as it is dominated by men. These factors also act as key barriers and obstacles to women's active participation in the Indian electoral system and in the larger issue of women's advancement as a whole.

Illiteracy

One of the main barriers to the participation of women in politics in this country is illiteracy. India has one of the largest illiterate populations. Illiteracy limits the ability of women to understand the political system and issues. Due to illiteracy, many women are sometimes left off the voter's list and, as a result, they are not able to exercise their political rights. Women who are into active politics and are not educated are not able to handle the office efficiently as the women who are educated have access to all sources of communication like memos and newspapers which helps them to be updated with all the latest news which helps them to make a wise political decision.

Finance and Economic problems

Poverty is another barrier that has led to the low political participation of women in India. Often poor people have no direct voting stance. It is often influenced by rich and well-off people. Just before elections, the poor people are given resources such as blankets, television, food, and alcohol by various political party workers so that these people vote in favor of them. There are various political parties that work for the poor people and there are some political groups and parties that only work for these groups. These political parties don't win easily as they are low in their funds if compared to other political parties who get their funding from rich business tycoons. Rich business tycoons invest in the parties from which they will get adequate returns. But these poor people shall get no returns as they do not pay that much tax that the other citizens of the country pay who are better off than these poor people.

Family barriers

Marriage is another barrier that leads to less political participation of women in India. After a woman gets married, all her political decisions are controlled by the family she is married into if she comes from an uneducated family. Even if she comes from an educated family to an extent she is influenced by the family she is married to and often there is a clash in ideology. After getting married, the woman has hardly any time to contest elections or go for campaigns as she has new responsibilities added to her shoulders. She needs to look after her family, she needs to look after the kids, needs to do all the household work, and even go to work.

Conclusion and suggestion

The Women's Reservation Bill seeks to amend the constitution to set aside for women one-third of all seats in the Lok Sabha, India's lower house, as well as in all state legislatures. Yet the bill has languished despite passing the Rajya Sabha, India's upper house, in 2010, a delay described by one study as showing a "lack of seriousness among political parties in taking better account of women's increasing electoral participation".

The failing goes beyond politics to community attitudes. A patriarchal mindset is still evident.

It is the need of the hour in a country like India to have equal participation of women in mainstream political activity. Society needs to deconstruct the stereotype of women as limited to household activities only. Overall political parties' environment too is not women-friendly, they have to struggle hard and face multi-dimensional issues to create space for themselves in the party. it is important for all institutions (state, family, and community) to respond to women's specific needs such as bridging gaps in education, renegotiating gender roles, the gender division of labor, and addressing biased attitudes

Notes

"*Every word a woman writes changes the story of the world, revises the official version.*

~Carolyn See"

Literature

by:- Sanchi Singla

VI
Literature

Industrialization and urbanization also made

Indian writers are aware of the world around them. Science and rationalism played a key part in modern Indian literature as Indian writers began to question certain institutions and norms.

Rather than attacking the themes of pre-modern

Indian literature (centered around themes of other-worldliness), modern Indian literature created new gods in their current society, the gods being man and nature.

Indian literature was formed during the anti-colonial movement against British imperialism in India. indian writers used Western forms of writing such as essays, drama, and fiction to tell their stories and represent the Indian experience.

Tagore was the first Indian to receive a Nobel prize for writing. in his play 'Bisorjon' (1890), he presented how following previous conventions were unrealistic and no longer served a purpose. in his poem, 'Gitanjali' (1910), the line below is reminiscent of hope not just for

the individual but hope for the whole nation of India.

1947, India entered an era of disenchantment due to Muslim Hindu riots and the murder of Mahatma Gandhi which led to the division of the country into India and Pakistan.

Dalit writers followed the teachings of their first modern Dalit leader, B. R. Ambedkar, in their writing. They criticized the caste system of India and the injustices they had to face being Dalit people and questioned the notion of rebirth in the Hindu caste system.

The quote *WE HAVE TO CHANGE THE SUN

ABOVE US* highlights just how deep-rooted the caste system was in Indian society.

Literature also started due to the British government's education reforms in India, missionary work, and the response to English literature and language from upper-class Indian people.

The best Dalit authors introduced not only a new substance but also a revolutionary new language, which drew pictures and metaphors of the non-Daiit world unknown to people in life.

in India, South Asia, Africa, and certain parts of the world, literary magazines may have another role to play. Support writing careers. The magazines are a pillar to graduates of literature, passionate readers, bibliophiles, and hobbyists; sending them the shoulder to spring start a probable writing career.

A rich literary magazine landscape comments on writing being taken seriously, and also nurtures a reading market for aspiring writers. Stimulating intellectual conversations, niche catering, lending support to Creative Writing programs, and providing a platform to be heard, or well, read; surround the larger role of magazines.

India and religion are connected with each other. indian literature is also influenced by religion.

Literature in the Indian context, beginning from times immemorial would never have been possible without the profound impression of religious and spiritual aspects. 'Vedas' is the most ancient Indian literature. The Puranas and two great epics, Ramayana and Mahabharata hold considerable significance even today.

Religious influence upon Indian literature made a transition from oral to written. Hindu mythology portrays the deities Brahma, Vishnu, and Shiva.

This mythology has influenced Indian literary texts, from Sanskrit literature to modern literature in Indian English. This influence continues even to the present day. The great Indian epics Ramayana and Mahabharata transcend the description of mere classics. They are a source of unfailing and everlasting inspiration. We have learned the whole way of our life — our manners, our morality, and our ethics from these epics. They have guided and sustained us over times immemorial, through our triumphs and failures, hopes and despairs, and have shown us the right way of life. Both these epics have always fascinated Indian novelists.

In Indian English fiction, it is the most popular discussed theme which is scarcely and difficult to disregard or overlook. It has influenced each part of Indian English Fiction. Literature and rural narrative are still left untold at certain closures thus I might want to make an unassuming endeavor to re-inventing the rural narratives in the light of Indian English Literature. The present thesis is an endeavor to analyze the village writings almost completely known in the realm of Indian fiction in English. The whole Indian English writings can be partitioned into two parts most definitely Pre and Post-independence periods.

Notes

WOMEN HELPLINE

WOMEN HELPLINE NUMBERS

Women Helpline (All India) -

Women In Distress:- 1091

Women Helpline Domestic Abuse:- 181

Police:- 100

National Commission For Women (NCW) (Domestic violence 24x7 helpline for Sexual Violence and harassment):- 7827170170

National Commission For Women (NCW):- 011-26942369, 26944754

Delhi Commission For Women:- 011-23378044 / 23378317 / 23370597

Outer Delhi Helpline:- 011-27034873, 27034874

Student / Child Helpline:- 1098

National Human Right Commission:- 011-23385368/:- 9810298900

Disclaimer

This book may contain some hard incidence, sentences, or words that can harm you or disturb you either mentally or emotionally. But that's not the intention behind writing this book. The author just wanted to bring out the problems and solutions as much as possible so that it could reach out to a maximum number of people which could help them to cover up from the hardships they have been dealing with.

I apologize beforehand for hurting your feelings as well as express gratitude for accepting this book as it is.

This book is based on true incidents as recorded by the victims who have suffered and wanted to bring change not only in their life but in every part of society.

About The Author

<u>Think positive and Stay Happy.</u>

Alleviate yourself and Make yourself proud one day. I am Sidaanti Singla presently studying law. I am writing this book because I like to help all those who have been facing difficulties in making themselves confident.

I have helped many of my friends when they faced the same. I am a good listener and people feel comfortable around me. They share their problems with me.

I also actively do yoga and exercise to keep myself calm and focused. I don't believe in any caste, religion or any other community divisions.

If any of you wishes to get in touch with me to lift you up, please feel free to contact me by using the link below.

My top influencers are my parents, comrades, family, instructors and me myself.

With lots of love

Sidaanti Singla

CONNECT TO THE AUTHOR

E-mail:- sidaantisingla@gmai.com

Facebook:-www.facebook.com/
people'svoiceinmywords

Twitter:- www.twitter.com/sidaanti

Notes

NOTES

www.ingramcontent.com/pod-product-compliance
Lightning Source LLC
Chambersburg PA
CBHW031303130726
47988CB00007B/2713